The Life and Work of...

Henri Matisse

Paul Flux

Heinemann Library
Chicago, Illinois

Designed by Celia Floyd
Illustrations by Karin Littlewood
Originated by Ambassador Litho Ltd.
Printed and bound in Hong Kong/China

06 05 04
10 9 8 7 6 5 4 3 2

Library of Congress Cataloging-in-Publication Data
Flux, Paul, 1952-
　Henri Matisse / Paul Flux.
　　　p. cm. -- (The life and work of...)
Includes bibliographical references and index.
Summary: Presents a brief overview of the life and work of this French
artist, describing and giving examples of his work.
　ISBN 1-58810-604-7 (lib.bdg.)　　ISBN 1-4034-0002-4 (pbk. bdg.)
　1. Matisse, Henri, 1869-1954--Juvenile literature. 2.
Artists--France--Biography--Juvenile literature. [1. Matisse, Henri,
1869-1954. 2. Artists. 3. Painting, French.] I. Title. II. Series.
　N6853.M33 F54 2002
　759.4--dc21
　　　　　　　　　　　　　2001003970

Acknowledgments
The author and publishers are grateful to the following for permission to reproduce copyright material:
pp. 4, 7, 13, 16, Bridgeman Art Library; p. 5, Albright Knox Art Gallery, Buffalo, New York; pp. 8, 10, Hulton Archive; p. 9, Hermitage, St. Petersburg, Russia; p. 11, Museum of Modern Art, New York, Mrs. Simon Guggenheim Fund; p. 12, Corbis; p. 15, CNAC/MNAN/RMN; p. 17, Christies Images; p. 18, Mary Evans Picture Library; p. 19, Pushkin Museum, Moscow; p. 21, Scottish National Gallery of Modern Art, Edinburgh; p. 23, Phillips Collection, Washington; p. 25, Chapelle di Rosaire, Venice; p. 26, AKG; pp. 27, 29, Succession H. Matisse/DACS 2002; p. 28, Magnum Photos.

Cover photograph (*The Fall of Icarus,* Henri Matisse) reproduced with permission of Succession H. Matisse/DACS.

Special thanks to Katie Miller for her comments in the preparation of this book.

Every effort has been made to contact copyright holders of any material reproduced in this book. Any omissions will be rectified in subsequent printings if notice is given to the publisher.

Some words are shown in bold, **like this.** You can find out what they mean by looking in the glossary.

Contents

Who Was Henri Matisse?

Henri Matisse was a French artist. His work is still very popular. He was one of the best painters of the 1900s.

Henri painted many different things in his life. This is one of his best known pictures. Henri loved to use bright colors and strong lines.

The Music, 1939

Early Years

Henri Matisse was born on December 31, 1869, on his grandfather's farm in France. He showed little interest in art while he was in school. He left school in 1887 to study **law** in Paris.

In 1890, when he was 21, Henri became very ill. His mother bought him a box of paints to cheer him up. He used them to paint pictures like this one.

Still-Life with Books and Candle, 1890

Love and Marriage

In 1892 Henri met Amélie Parayre. They fell in love. In 1894, Henri's first child was born. He and Amélie had two more children and lived in Paris.

Henri and Amélie were married in 1898. Henri painted this picture of his wife many years later. He often used her as a **model** for his paintings.

Portrait of the Artist's Wife, 1913

Teaching Art

In 1907, Henri opened his own art school. It was very popular. He had to close the school in 1911, though. Henri's 60 students were taking too much time away from his work.

Henri tried using color in new ways. He painted this picture of his own **studio**. This was unlike any painting he had ever done before.

The Red Studio, 1911

In the United States

In 1913, Henri was asked to show his work in New York, which is shown here. People had rarely seen such **abstract** and colorful pictures. The paintings did not look like anything in real life.

A lot of people did not like Henri's paintings. They thought his work was too bright and hard to understand. In Chicago, Illinois, people burned a copy of one of his paintings to show how much they disliked it.

Interior with Aubergines, 1911

War Breaks Out

In 1914, **World War I** began. Henri had many of his paintings hanging at an **exhibition** in Berlin. They were all taken by the German **government**.

Henri painted this picture after the war had begun. He painted darkness to show it was a time when many people were frightened.

French Window at Collioure, 1914

Henri and Pablo Picasso

In 1918, Henri had a big **exhibition** with Pablo Picasso, another great artist. The two men painted very differently, but they **admired** each other's work.

16

During the 1920s, Henri grew more famous. He kept searching for better ways to paint. In 1925, he was given the Legion of Honor as an award from the French **government**.

Woman Reading, 1922

Another War

In 1939, **World War II** began. Soon there were lots of German soldiers in France. Henri left Paris and went back to southern France.

In 1939, Henri **separated** from Amélie, but he still thought about her. He also was worried by the terrible war. The black background in this picture shows his troubled mood.

Still-Life with a Seashell on Black Marble, 1940

The War Years

During the war, Henri became very ill. He had to stay in bed for nearly a year. He was never in good health again.

This picture was finished when the war was at its worst. It shows the myth of **Icarus,** the man who flew too close to the Sun. Henri wanted to show how fighting could **destroy** good ideas.

The Fall of Icarus, 1947

21

A Troubled Time

In April 1944, the German secret police **arrested** Henri's wife and his daughter, Marguerite. They were sent to jail for helping the fight against the Germans. Henri was very worried about them.

Amélie and Marguerite were set free after many months in jail. Although he was worried and unwell, Henri continued to paint. For several years, many of his paintings showed his fears for his family and country.

The Egyptian Curtain, 1948

The Chapel in Vence

In 1947, Henri was visited by a nun. She had cared for him when he had been ill. She showed him a **design** she had made for a new church window. Henri decided to design a whole new **chapel**.

24

Henri took this work very seriously. It took them four years to finish the chapel in Vence, France. This is a window Henri designed for the chapel.

Tree of Life, 1951

Failing Health

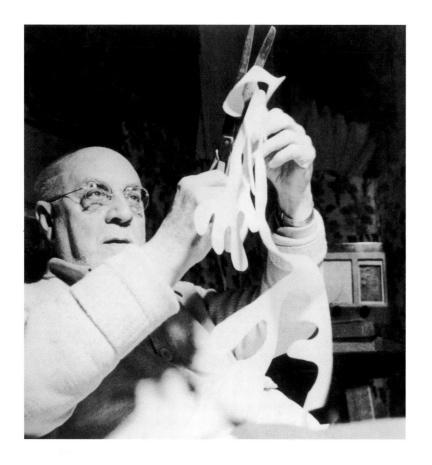

Soon Henri became too ill to paint. He started using **cut-out** pieces of colored paper to make his pictures. Other people helped him. He found the different results exciting.

Many of Henri's cut-outs show that life is enjoyable. But some were made to show sadness. This painting shows what an unhappy king sees.

Sorrows of the King, 1952

Last Days

Henri continued to work even though he was becoming very weak. He was working on a **design** for a church window when he died on November 3, 1954.

Henri used color in ways no one had ever tried before. Even in his last works, he used bright colors that seemed full of life. Henri was truly a great artist.

The Snail, 1953

Timeline

1869	Henri Matisse is born on December 31, in France.
1887	Henri studies **law** in Paris.
1892	He begins to study painting in the **studio** of Gustave Moreau.
1898	Amélie Parayre and Henri are married.
1904	Henri has his first one-man show.
1907	Henri opens his own art school in Paris. He meets Pablo Picasso for the first time.
1913	Henri shows his work in New York.
1914	Henri has paintings in an **exhibition** in Berlin. When war begins, these paintings are taken by the German **government**.
1917	The artist Edgar Degas dies.
1918	Picasso and Matisse hold a big exhibition together.
1927	Henri is given the painting prize at the Carnegie Exhibition.
1939	**World War II** breaks out.
1941	Henri is very ill, but he returns to work.
1944	His wife and daughter are **arrested**.
1945	World War II ends.
1947	Henri begins work on the **chapel** in Vence, France.
1952	The Matisse Museum is set up at his place of birth.
1954	Henri dies on November 3.

Glossary

abstract kind of art that does not try to show people or things. It uses shape and color to make the picture.

admire to think something or someone is very good

arrested caught by the police

chapel small part of a larger church

cut-out piece of paper that has been cut into a shape

design plan or drawing of something

destroy break or ruin

exhibition public display of works of art

government people who control a country

Icarus man in Greek myth who escaped from prison using wings his father had made. Icarus died when he flew too close to the Sun and the wax in his wings melted.

law rules of a country

model person who poses for an artist to draw or paint

separate split up, as in a marriage

studio room or building where an artist works

World War I war in Europe that lasted from 1914 to 1918

World War II war fought in Europe, Africa, and Asia from 1939 to 1945

Index

More Books to Read

Le Tord, Bijou. *A Bird or Two.* Grand Rapids, Mich.: Eerdmans, 1999.

O'Connor. *Henri Matisse.* New York: Penguin Putnam, 2002.

Venezia, Mike. *Henri Matisse.* Danbury, Conn.: Children's Press, 1997.

More Artwork to See

Open Window, Collioure. 1905. National Gallery of Art, Washington, D.C.

Promenade among the Olive Trees. 1906. Metropolitan Museum of Art, New York, N.Y.

White Plumes. 1919. Minneapolis Institute of Arts, Minnesota